STEVE WATERS

Steve Waters' plays include *Why Can't We Live Together?*
(Menagerie Theatre/Soho/Theatre503); *Europa*, as co-author
(Birmingham Repertory Theatre/Dresden State Theatre/Teatr
Polski Bydgoszcz/Zagreb Youth Theatre); *Ignorance/Jahiliyyah*
(Hampstead Downstairs); *Little Platoons*, *The Contingency
Plan*, *Capernaum*, part of *Sixty-Six Books* (Bush, London); *Fast
Labour* (Hampstead, in association with West Yorkshire
Playhouse); *Out of Your Knowledge* (Menagerie Theatre/
Pleasance, Edinburgh/East Anglian tour); *World Music*
(Sheffield Crucible, and subsequent transfer to the Donmar
Warehouse); *The Unthinkable* (Sheffield Crucible); *English
Journeys*, *After the Gods* (Hampstead); a translation/adaptation
of a new play by Philippe Minyana, *Habitats* (Gate, London/
Tron, Glasgow); *Flight Without End* (LAMDA). Writing for
television and radio includes *Safe House* (BBC4), *The Air Gap*,
The Moderniser (BBC Radio 4), *Scribblers* and *Bretton Woods*
(BBC Radio 3). Steve ran the Birmingham MPhil in
Playwriting for several years and from autumn 2015 will run
the MA Creative Writing: Script at the University of East
Anglia. He is the author of *The Secret Life of Plays*, also
published by Nick Hern Books.

Other Titles in this Series

Mike Bartlett
BULL
GAME
AN INTERVENTION
KING CHARLES III

Jez Butterworth
JERUSALEM
JEZ BUTTERWORTH PLAYS: ONE
MOJO
THE NIGHT HERON
PARLOUR SONG
THE RIVER
THE WINTERLING

Caryl Churchill
BLUE HEART
CHURCHILL PLAYS: THREE
CHURCHILL PLAYS: FOUR
CHURCHILL: SHORTS
CLOUD NINE
DING DONG THE WICKED
A DREAM PLAY *after* Strindberg
DRUNK ENOUGH TO SAY
    I LOVE YOU?
FAR AWAY
HOTEL
ICECREAM
LIGHT SHINING IN
    BUCKINGHAMSHIRE
LOVE AND INFORMATION
MAD FOREST
A NUMBER
SEVEN JEWISH CHILDREN
THE SKRIKER
THIS IS A CHAIR
THYESTES *after* Seneca
TRAPS

Stella Feehily
BANG BANG BANG
DREAMS OF VIOLENCE
DUCK
O GO MY MAN
THIS MAY HURT A BIT

debbie tucker green
BORN BAD
DIRTY BUTTERFLY
HANG
NUT
RANDOM
STONING MARY
TRADE & GENERATIONS
TRUTH AND RECONCILIATION

Anna Jordan
CHICKEN SHOP
FREAK
YEN

Lucy Kirkwood
BEAUTY AND THE BEAST
    with Katie Mitchell
BLOODY WIMMIN
CHIMERICA
HEDDA *after* Ibsen
IT FELT EMPTY WHEN THE
    HEART WENT AT FIRST BUT
    IT IS ALRIGHT NOW
NSFW
TINDERBOX

Conor McPherson
DUBLIN CAROL
McPHERSON PLAYS: ONE
McPHERSON PLAYS: TWO
McPHERSON PLAYS: THREE
THE NIGHT ALIVE
PORT AUTHORITY
THE SEAFARER
SHINING CITY
THE VEIL
THE WEIR

Jack Thorne
2ND MAY 1997
BUNNY
BURYING YOUR BROTHER IN THE
    PAVEMENT
HOPE
JACK THORNE PLAYS: ONE
LET THE RIGHT ONE IN
    after John Ajvide Lindqvist
MYDIDAE
STACY & FANNY AND FAGGOT
WHEN YOU CURE ME

Enda Walsh
BALLYTURK
BEDBOUND & MISTERMAN
DELIRIUM
DISCO PIGS & SUCKING DUBLIN
ENDA WALSH PLAYS: ONE
ENDA WALSH PLAYS: TWO
MISTERMAN
THE NEW ELECTRIC BALLROOM
ONCE
PENELOPE
THE SMALL THINGS
ROALD DAHL'S THE TWITS
THE WALWORTH FARCE

Steve Waters
THE CONTINGENCY PLAN
FAST LABOUR
IGNORANCE/JAHILIYYAH
LITTLE PLATOONS
THE UNTHINKABLE
WORLD MUSIC

Steve Waters

TEMPLE

NICK HERN BOOKS

London

www.nickhernbooks.co.uk

A Nick Hern Book

Temple first published in Great Britain in 2015 as a paperback original by Nick Hern Books Limited, The Glasshouse, 49a Goldhawk Road, London W12 8QP

Temple copyright © 2015 Steve Waters

Steve Waters has asserted his moral right to be identified as the author of this work

Cover image: Simon Russell Beale as The Dean; photography by Michele Turrani; artwork by AKA

Designed and typeset by Nick Hern Books, London
Printed in Great Britain by CPI Group (UK) Ltd

A CIP catalogue record for this book is available from the British Library

ISBN   978 1 84842 475 3

Temple was first performed at the Donmar Warehouse, London, on 27 May 2015 (previews from 21 May), with the following cast:

THE PA	Rebecca Humphries
THE DEAN	Simon Russell Beale
THE CANON CHANCELLOR	Paul Higgins
THE VIRGER	Anna Calder-Marshall
THE BISHOP OF LONDON	Malcolm Sinclair
THE CITY LAWYER	Shereen Martin

Director	Howard Davies
Designer	Tim Hatley
Lighting Designer	Mark Henderson
Sound Designer	Mike Walker
Composer	Stephen Warbeck
Casting Director	Alastair Coomer CDG

Acknowledgements

The author would like to thank the following people:

Doreen Chalmers, Reverend Giles Fraser, Reverend Canon Michael Hampel, Reverend Doctor James Hawkey, Right Reverend Graeme Knowles, Right Reverend Canon Mark Oakley, Professor Peter McCullough, Stephanie Norris.

None of the opinions expressed in the play are attributable to them.

Thanks to all the Donmar, especially Josie Rourke and Kate Pakenham, to Howard Davies and all the cast of the original production for their help in developing the play.

S.W.

For my parents, Derek and Yvonne Waters

'…Some presage of an act
Which our eyes are compelled to witness, has forced our feet
Towards the cathedral.'

T.S. Eliot, Murder in the Cathedral

Characters

THE DEAN, *male, fifties*
THE CANON CHANCELLOR, *male, forties*
THE PA, *female, twenties*
THE VIRGER, *female, sixties*
THE BISHOP OF LONDON, *male, sixties*
LAWYER FOR THE CORPORATION OF THE CITY OF
    LONDON, *female, thirties*
TWO CHORISTERS, *male, ten*

Setting

The Chapter House by St Paul's Cathedral.

This play is an imagined version of real events. Characters have been invented or reinvented, events telescoped and modified.

This text went to press before the end of rehearsals and so may differ slightly from the play as performed.

From somewhere comes the sound of a choir singing 'Te Deum Laudamus' as set by Thomas Tallis.

The Chapter House, 9 a.m., Friday October 28th, 2011.

A large reception room, panelled walls with a series of tall sash windows facing out onto the north side of the cathedral; the room is on the first storey. There are portraits of the former Deans of St Paul's from John Moses to John Donne hanging on the wall; a rather gilded mirror; a chandelier hangs from the ceiling. On the right of the room, a bookshelf rises from floor to ceiling accessed by a wooden stepladder; it is full of works of theology, variants of the Bible, service orders, the Book of Common Prayer *and so on. The floor is stripped back to boards with a central thick carpet.*

The centre of the room is dominated by a long table for a meeting. Incongruously on a side table is a kettle and a series of grubby mugs with tea items; a plate with cling film over it holds some depleted-looking biscuits. Also there are papers laid out as if for a meeting, in some state of disarray; the odd wrapping from a food item, coffee cups; the chairs are in a disordered state too and there is a flip chart with a number of notes and numbers on it.

The door stage right leads off to the corridor and the entry.

Through the windows autumn light, pale and cool, streams; there's a confused sense of a presence beyond the palings and a low hum of noise, the odd whistle and cheer. The bells ring for nine o'clock.

The DEAN *enters in an overcoat with scarf and gloves. He stands taken aback by the state of the room and makes as if to begin to tidy. This comes to nothing. He unknots his scarf slowly; drifts to the window; there is a sudden strange muffled sound as if a tiny pocket choir were singing; the* DEAN *gets*

*into a slightly frantic business of extricating what it becomes
apparent is his phone from his coat; its ringtone is Tallis's
'Spem in Alium'; instinctively he recoils from it, placing it on
the table as if it is a foreign object.*

*He looks at it. He switches it off. The silence is satisfying. Now
another phone goes – this time the ringtone is something
altogether funkier – somewhere amidst the papers on the table;
the DEAN locates it, silences it. Places it down thoughtfully,
takes off coat to reveal dog collar and dark shirt with poppy.*

*Now the PA storms in – a woman in her twenties; she is also in
a winter coat, slightly worn – her hair is pulled back from her
face and her make-up is a little uneven in application; she
carries an incongruously scruffy rucksack given her overall
look. She drops the rucksack, out of breath and almost unable
to speak.*

PA. You're already here.

DEAN. Of course.

PA. Sorry, ran from – Liverpool Street. Dodging – road blocks.

DEAN. Catch your breath.

PA. Yes.

She breathes hard.

Sorry, is it okay if I – ?

*She rummages in her rucksack and pulls out an inhaler and
takes a puff.*

Better. Ah. Shouldn't…

*Now she gets a fit of coughing and rummages; the DEAN
makes as if to help but she waves him off and finds some
water and glugs greedily. Which makes her cough more.*

Really wanted to pre-empt you – getting in, Dean.

DEAN. It's 'Mr Dean'. Actually.

PA. 'Mr Dean'?

DEAN. If we are to use the correct nomenclature.

PA. 'Mr Dean'.

Now the DEAN *starts to tidy rather ineffectually.*

No, no, don't you... I should be –

She joins in.

Need some sort of black sack, really.

She exits off. He stands rather confused with some cups. She re-enters with a sack, takes the cups.

I suppose, in my defence, I slightly thought – with you ending so late last night – as I understand it –

DEAN. It was certainly late, yes.

PA. I suppose I thought you might have come in... a little later today.

DEAN. Oh. Oh I see. That I might have had a, what, a lie-in?

Cancel Morning Prayers perhaps?

PA. Well, okay... just, you know, given the church is actually – closed.

DEAN. No, no I begin to see the logic. You imagined, quite reasonably I suppose that we might, what, 'reschedule' – that we might push back the time-immemorial burden of worship, the commencement of the day's liturgical tasks which begin at an inconveniently prompt hour and of course where would be the harm in that? I think only eight of us were there and all in email contact – and God exists largely outside time as we understand it.

PA. I'm sorry – that was probably hugely – ignorant.

DEAN. You come from the Development I think? Fund-raising? Well, during your time in Development you'll have acquired the misplaced notion of St Paul's as a workplace. A place of work. And yes it appears in so many respects I would imagine from your vantage point as a 'job', a job of work in a recognisably modern organisation, subject to contemporary expectations of work/life balance and Equal Opportunities, and we do aspire to that, we are not entirely antediluvian – oh, now I had better get on, really. This needs to be readied for the Press Reception at I think –

PA. 12.30?

DEAN. No, that's Eucharist.

PA. My mistake – 1.30.

DEAN. You have the press office's number?

PA. I've got a whole pack of contacts and – just processing it –

DEAN. I was told you'd be thoroughly briefed – well, we'll need a round-robin to all staff –

PA. Great. So basically chapter?

DEAN. To the entire two hundred and fifty members of our staff –

PA. Got you –

DEAN. – a round-robin to the effect that we will reopen the cathedral for worship today at Eucharist.

PA. At 12.30.

DEAN. Indeed. And summarise these notes. In my hopefully legible hand.

He hands her a notebook.

PA. So these are, sorry – the minutes? From last night.

DEAN. It was a closed meeting.

PA. Okay. Okay. Well, I expect I'll be able to… make them out –

She leafs through the tiny notebook. He waits. She looks at him.

The thing is I commute. From Royston. And we had to get a replacement bus? From Hitchin –

Suddenly she's in tears.

And obviously I know about Morning Prayers, my dad's a vicar for fuck's sake. Oh God. And now I just swore.

And then I – blasphemed.

DEAN. It's fine.

PA. No, it's *so* not fine.

She weeps quietly. He stands.

DEAN. I don't know your name. They told it me and I…

PA (*almost inaudible*). Lizzie.

DEAN. 'Lizzie'. You say your father's a vicar?

PA. I mean I would completely understand if you wanted me to – do you want me to go? I'm sure she, thingy, Barbara, you could probably get her in again.

DEAN. Barbara! Barbara is suffering from nervous exhaustion and is unlikely to be with us for some time. The straw that broke the dromedary's back was her being called a very ugly word for a very private part of the female anatomy – was it by the Religious Affairs Correspondent for Sky? Can such a person even exist? So you are not only now working for an anachronistic organisation in terms of norms and expectations, you are also working for an ailing institution in – oh, I do find people to be very fragile these days.

Not that I exclude myself…

A phone rings off.

Forgive me. For speaking with such… asperity. So often this last week I've found myself speaking like a person I do not recognise.

PA. It's really not a problem. I interned at a wealth-management place, off Cheapside. They called me the 'Chavette'. I should probably get that?

The DEAN *seems far away. She goes.*

The CANON CHANCELLOR *enters in jeans and a woolly jumper with a plastic bag of books.*

DEAN. What is that song they always sing?

CANON CHANCELLOR. Sorry?

DEAN. The song they always sing. Whenever two or three gather together and a guitar is to hand?

CANON CHANCELLOR. 'Kumbaya'?

He's looking for something.

DEAN. I have no quarrel with 'Kumbaya'.

No, this ditty, or is it a mantra, simply goes on and on, drones on, forlorn yet ostensibly hopeful, if the lyrics, such as they are, are to be treated seriously.

'Everything's gonna be alright, everything's gonna be alright, everything's gonna be alright, everything's gonna be alright.'

Words to that effect. Are you looking for this?

He gives the CANON CHANCELLOR *the smartphone.*

CANON CHANCELLOR. Deo gratias!

DEAN. A theological overstatement perhaps?

CANON CHANCELLOR. Fifty missed calls.

DEAN. Ah. Your eager public?

The CANON CHANCELLOR *looks oddly at the* DEAN.

CANON CHANCELLOR. I brought back some of your lendings. Mr Dean.

DEAN. Oh. No necessity for that yet, surely. Canon Chancellor.

CANON CHANCELLOR. Had to pass the night somehow, hardly going to sleep. Rummaging through a whole archive of sermons, papers, stuff; don't know if St Paul's wants any of that. Probably straight in the shredder.

DEAN. Everything that passed between us last night remains confidential.

CANON CHANCELLOR. I'm sorry? Little thick-headed I
warn you, too much – coffee.

DEAN. I mean I retain my hope that we might remain... intact.
As a chapter. That you might reconsider your decision.

The CANON CHANCELLOR *is speechless for a moment.*

CANON CHANCELLOR. Yeah, anyway. Barth. *Church
Dogmatics.* Volume Three, for some reason. Always assumed
it was mine, but that's your handwriting, immaculate
copperplate. And your 'Shape of the Liturgy' I think. This
volume of some of Rowan's more challenging free verse,
mmm, signed copy. Probably worth something.

DEAN. I do find contemporary poetry lacking in – discipline.

CANON CHANCELLOR *hauls himself up the ladder to
inspect the bookshelves.*

I expect you won't feel able to look over this press release?

CANON CHANCELLOR. Doubt that's even appropriate.

DEAN. You are still in our employ, I think.

CANON CHANCELLOR. Might inveigle something in it
foreign to our – your – direction of travel.

DEAN. You're very sure of our direction of travel.

CANON CHANCELLOR. Did something shift last night after I
skedaddled? Sudden lurch to the left?

DEAN. Left, right – it's hardly so simple.

The PA *enters. The bells ring the quarter-hour.*

PA. Oh, sorry.

DEAN. It's fine, it's fine.

CANON CHANCELLOR. Pretend I'm not here. Works for
everyone else.

PA. I expect I don't open post. Just a heads-up on quite a
weirdy-looking one...

DEAN. May I see?

PA. I never get letters. (*To* CANON CHANCELLOR.) I'm Lizzie.

CANON CHANCELLOR. I think we've met. But 'welcome', nevertheless.

DEAN. They don't get any less hateful.

'You're damned for what you did, vicar; damned for giving into (expletive) sickos (psychos?) and tramps.'

CANON CHANCELLOR. Not another green-ink nutjob?

DEAN. 'Damned for closing the greatest church on earth.'

As in 'D-A-M-M-E-D'. The spelling's more offensive than the sentiments.

Unsigned, of course.

CANON CHANCELLOR. Bastards. I'm sorry but – witless, ignorant – bastards.

PA. Well, sorry to be the bearer of –

Pause.

So I had a stab at the minutes but I got a bit flummoxed as to the action points? I sense chapter came to a vote to reopen the cathedral. Or was it to seek a legal injunction against Occupy? Or maybe, maybe both?

I'm probably being really dim.

CANON CHANCELLOR. Such an elegant impasse: some of us ready to water-cannon Occupy into the Fleet; some of us tangled up in liberal qualms; me, on my high horse – you magnificently above the fray.

DEAN. I've never considered it my task to coerce chapter one way or another.

CANON CHANCELLOR. Heaven forfend you might offer anything as vulgar as leadership!

Yet who wields the casting vote?

DEAN. The complexion of any vote as you well know is confidential.

CANON CHANCELLOR. Of course. So you're not having second thoughts?

Pause.

PA. Okay. So I guess I need to know what you want me to write – in the round-robin?

DEAN. Simply state that chapter met last night, and reached agreement in its intent that we reopen for worship today. The rest of our deliberations – and their consequences – we will address in our press briefing at 1.30.

CANON CHANCELLOR. Which'll seriously beg some questions.

DEAN. No doubt.

CANON CHANCELLOR. Last week we told the world we *so* had to close St Paul's, unprecedented act, heavy heart, can't possibly run this *iconic* building with all those hippies and hackers on our porch – oh no sir, health and safety, multiple trip hazards, all of that –

DEAN. I really don't know why you adopt this satiric tone –

CANON CHANCELLOR. A week later, mirabile dictu, we're open for business after all – oh and not 'cause we're shedding twenty-two K a day, oh no – and okay, they're still there the hippy hackers; course we'll not sully ourselves by talking to them, oh no, steady on – but neither do we have the guts to admit we'd like them bundled in a Black Maria –

DEAN. Lizzie, could you leave us please?

PA. Sure, for sure. Just I'm presuming – opening the sure –

The PA *goes.*

DEAN. You're evidently steadfast in your intent to leave.

CANON CHANCELLOR. Did you think I resigned out of some sort of hissy fit?

DEAN. Fine, fine. I recognise you are now flexing your muscles, relishing your new freedom of manoeuvre and so forth but I have to tell you I do not find your presence or your observations in any sense helpful or I am sad to say – pleasurable. Right now.

CANON CHANCELLOR. Yeah. Okay. Got that.

He's searching for something on his phone.

DEAN. I need to ready myself.

CANON CHANCELLOR. Occupy Oakland – California.

DEAN. Yes, I know where Oakland is.

CANON CHANCELLOR. You see the cops lined up here, and here's Occupy, outside City Hall. This is last night. Little grainy figure's a soldier. Done a tour or two in Iraq I believe. A sort of informal figurehead, of course they don't like the term 'leader'. Twenty-four. Okay, and here – ouch.

The phone emits a rather confused noise; the DEAN *looks away.*

That's got to hurt. Yeah, essentially they fire a tear-gas canister into his face. No warning given. Brain swelling, fractured cranium.

DEAN. Very – unfortunate.

CANON CHANCELLOR. Isn't it just?

DEAN. Makes one grateful for the good judgement of our police.

CANON CHANCELLOR. Ah. 'Isolated case'; okay, you can see here the police in law-abiding Melbourne, removing Occupy from the City Square –

He plays a rather scratchy YouTube clip.

Mmm, here we go, pepper spray, eye-gouging, punches to the head and face – even to kids apparently –

DEAN. Do you think perhaps your interest in this borders on the pathological?

The CANON CHANCELLOR *is astonished.*

CANON CHANCELLOR. Well very possibly, very – possibly. But if we're talking pathology we might mention your denial of what you'll unleash if you stand by this decision. Will you – stand by it?

Pause.

DEAN. Don't neglect to retrieve your own books.

All those works of continental philosophy lent with heavy hints – was it René Girard? I regret I couldn't get past the first chapter. Yoder? Faith subordinate to social action. Out of patience even with the preface. So sorry – to disappoint.

CANON CHANCELLOR. No especial hurry. To have them back.

DEAN. Of course as you work out your notice we will continue to value any contribution you can make in the difficult days ahead; given the pressures we face today I would particularly value your discretion – we will announce your decision to leave us at the press conference this afternoon. Can I count on this – discretion? Until that time?

The VIRGER, *a woman with silver hair cropped short and a severe dark suit, enters.*

CANON CHANCELLOR. Morning, Michelle. Prayers go with a swing?

VIRGER. Nothing more pointless than an empty cathedral. Like putting on a play day after day without an audience. Nobody's in reception.

The PA *enters.*

PA. Sorry. That was probably my – I probably –

VIRGER. I suppose I should offer congratulations. And commiserations.

CANON CHANCELLOR. Either refer to me?

VIRGER. Everyone's praying the situation with Barbara is temporary. Considering the many years she's given us. Not that that it counts for much these days.

PA. Okay. Well, thanks anyway for your – good wishes.

The bells ring the half-hour. The PA *goes.*

DEAN. Lizzie will of course need our support. As will our Canon Chancellor here. Our prayers.

CANON CHANCELLOR. Oh absolutely, every one of them. I'll piss off then – I take it I can get out the back way.

VIRGER. Blocked off by the police. You'll have to sneak out the front. I dare say you'll pass unnoticed amongst them.

CANON CHANCELLOR. I dare say.

DEAN. I hope you'll join us. For worship.

CANON CHANCELLOR. Worship at any cost. Nah, you don't really want me there, do you? In truth.

He goes.

VIRGER. So you finally decided?

You do realise we need at least a day's grace. At least.

DEAN. Whatever happens we will keep it low-key.

VIRGER. The Registrar wouldn't say either way. The Precentor muttered something about good and bad news which made no sense at all.

DEAN. We must ready ourselves for opening.

VIRGER. You cannot close a church for a fortnight and expect it ready for the public in the blink of an eye. There's unresolved issues of ingress and egress. We can't use the north transept, the crypt I presume remains shut, everyone coming through the west door – what about our unwashed friends on the portal? These things need risk-assessing – you'll delay it at least until Evensong?

DEAN. We – I – intend to celebrate Eucharist.

VIRGER. Eucharist! It will put us in a very poor light, again. We will appear great incompetents again and I know I am not alone in this –

DEAN. You have been clamouring – rightly – for this –

VIRGER. We haven't lacquered the candelabra, we've not washed the kneelers, we've not laundered the altar cloth – did chapter consider the fact of it being a feast day?

DEAN. Let the world see what closure has done to us –

VIRGER. Well. May I register my – disgust – at how this is being handled.

DEAN. 'Disgust' is an extremely strong word.

VIRGER. It's the word God granted me. Which is another reason – well, it's more coherent in here.

She hands him a note in an envelope.

I didn't feel email was appropriate.

DEAN. I sincerely hope this is not what it appears to be.

VIRGER. Seeing your predecessor, there, Dr Moses; the pain this would have caused him.

DEAN. I am sure of it.

VIRGER. Or Reverend Evans, my first dean. A perfect marriage of the spiritual and the worldly.

DEAN. A difficult balance to effect.

VIRGER. That's the church I joined, I loved. All said better in there – I don't entirely blame you. The cause is plain enough.

She goes to a window.

Moronic hand-painted banners: 'What would Jesus do?' Your heart goes out to the police, the abuse they get, all hours, and who's paying for it? I'll see today through of course.

DEAN. Michelle, I understand you have found my leadership at times perhaps lacking in certainty – perhaps you've found me, well, vacillating. That you would like to see a conviction in me, both spiritual and temporal, you imagine I do not possess – but leadership is not mere decision-making –

VIRGER. I really can't stay for this. Dean.

DEAN. I will not read this until you allow me the courtesy of discussing your –

VIRGER. There's no *time*.

DEAN. Then we shall make time.

VIRGER. The minor canons are saying you're thinking of preaching. I told them that couldn't possibly be correct.

She leaves. The DEAN *stands with the letter; then pockets it. He sits down, puts his face in his hands. We hear a police helicopter, very loud.*

He stands briskly, and ascends the ladder to the bookshelf with a sudden energy. The PA *comes in, then hangs back.*

PA. Sorry.

DEAN. Barbara was my first PA. I found it hard, accustoming myself to someone else answering my emails, governing my diary. But what I found especially hard was Barbara constantly enacting the drama of trespassing on my attention when that was actually her job. So please, may we have fewer apologies.

PA. Sorry. Oh. Mr Dean, the thing is –

DEAN. How's your history, Lizzie?

PA. Oh. I'm a history grad, actually. Well, history and politics.

DEAN. An apt combination.

PA. Technically I'm not a graduate; got glandular fever in my final year – my dissertation got a distinction. About witchcraft, but sort of through the lens of queer theory? 'Queering the Witch'?

DEAN. Fascinating. So you'll know Stow's *Survey of London*?

PA. Not ringing a bell. Could look it up on Ebo.

DEAN. I'd like the blueprint of the pre-Wren St Paul's – and any references you can find to the Paul's Cross – or the folk-meet – am I being arcane? I can be arcane.

PA. Not at all. Paul's Cross. Okay.

The PA*'s noting this down.*

Oh. The thing I came in for.

Basically, the Canon Chancellor's resigned.

DEAN. Well, that's hardly news.

PA. Yeah; no, I mean he's publically… resigned.

DEAN. How could he? He was just here.

PA. Tweeted his resignation at – yes – 9.35 a.m. – to be precise.

The bells ring the quarter-hour.

DEAN. You saw him. We spoke.

PA. Well, perhaps he then went off – to – tweet.

DEAN. But this was – minutes ago.

PA. Twitter's basically instantaneous. In impact.

Quite a terse one. Would you like to read it?

DEAN. I don't receive these things.

PA. Oh, anyone can read it. And given the traffic of calls we're getting everyone – has.

DEAN. Read it to me.

PA. Okay. 'It is with great regret and sadness that I have handed in my notice at St Paul's Cathedral.'

DEAN. Is that it?

PA. And another one: 'I resigned because I believe that the chapter is set on a course of action that could mean there will be violence in the name of the Church.'

DEAN. Convoluted, even for him. Isn't there a limit on these things?

PA. Just in at, yeah, one hundred and forty.

DEAN. 'A course of action'? A course of action yet to be confirmed.

PA. Is he maybe trying to leave you wriggle room –

DEAN. 'Violence in the name of the Church'? Paratroopers in cassocks perhaps? Prebends wielding fire hoses! Deacons riding shotgun in armoured personnel carriers – doesn't this tweet box us in? Doesn't this tweet make more possible what he fears?

PA. I guess it could be seen – it could be argued that he's maybe... calling you out? Or maybe saying it this way so you kind of have to – hear it? Or that maybe it creates an opportunity, a sort of space for you to clarify –

DEAN. Your esteem for him is not uncommon; I share it; I did appoint the man; but also you should be clear that it is the chapter which governs this church, that we, the chapter, function as a corporation, sole and entire, a body, and that we tirelessly, even tediously, seek to reach *agreement*, and that we defend and abide by our agreements, and thereby we supersede our individuality, and this is how we have always worked, because in this way we might reach something that approximates God's way and this tweet – this tweet – dashes that work to smithereens!

PA. Obviously, I'm not up to speed with... all the ins and outs.

DEAN. Either way I would be grateful for a little less unsolicited advice.

PA. Of course. Sorry.

DEAN. Yet I cannot anathematise him.

Now another ping on her device.

Another one? Flying around us, the air thronging with hostile, ill-considered thoughts.

PA. Mmm. Okay, it seems, hang on, there's already a campaign
    – oh – to reinstate him. Which slightly misunderstands what
    a resignation is.

DEAN. I suspect he suffers, yes, some sort of addiction to
    broadcast every thought and impulse – how does the world
    find the hours in the day to read and write all this –
    twittering?

PA. Oh, and yeah… and, also that was what the call was about –

DEAN. The call?

PA. Yes, just now – the Bishop of London, or the Bishop's team
    seem to have read it. I expect they were following him.

DEAN. The Bishop! Of course the Bishop would naturally be
    ahead of me on this. I expect the Bishop has someone
    tracking his own – what is it – 'web presence'? Should I put
    you on the task for me?

PA. I did google you. Very little came up.

DEAN. Delighted to hear it. Oh, so what does he want?

PA. He thinks it would be helpful if you met. And he'd be
    grateful as would I, if you switched on your mobile.

DEAN. I saw him not one hour ago, we are practically
    neighbours.

PA. He wonders if you want him at the press conference.

DEAN. What's enviable about the Bishop, and I say this in a
    spirit of affection, is the fact he is largely without portfolio, no
    dragging a building around for him, no, he springs up here,
    there, a royal wedding, a glamorous speaking assignment,
    utterly at liberty to be endlessly visible – an enviable condition
    which our newly departed colleague seems to aspire to – yes,
    very enviable when some of us instead must bear the weight
    of these great churches on our backs, but then without them do
    we not float around like spindrift?

The BISHOP *is there already, slightly déshabillé in a
Barbour jacket.*

BISHOP. If I were prone to suspicion I might imagine you were speaking of me. Good morning, both. Now, very good, this must be Barbara's temporary replacement?

DEAN. We pray not temporary.

PA. Yes. Hello. 'Your Grace'?

BISHOP. Please. Quite a step change. From the incumbent.

Welcome, welcome. Now, this is to be very quick as I have an, er, engagement – just something I need to confirm with you which as you refuse to deploy your phone you necessitate me addressing in person. With you *solus* I think.

The BISHOP *intimates they need to be alone, none too subtly.*

DEAN. Right. Lizzie, perhaps you could pop out for a coffee for myself and the Bishop? Just a black coffee for me.

PA. Right. Of course. Americano.

DEAN. I mean just an ordinary –

PA. Americano, yep. Sugar?

DEAN. Oh. Two.

PA. Bishop?

BISHOP. A flat white I think. Thank you.

The PA *goes.*

These days it's scarcely possible to walk down Paternoster Row without becoming engaged in the most fascinating wrangle of one sort or another. Have you visited the so-called University Tent? Quite remarkable debates about oh, fractional banking reserves, the notion of Jubilee, debt cancellation. Astonishing. Astonishingly interesting. Mmm. Insufficient rigour perhaps. And I question their stated commitment to recycling, the ubiquitous litter is very regrettable.

DEAN. Not to mention the human excrement in the North Churchyard.

BISHOP. I'm reminded of Marcel Mauss. You know Mauss's
    work?

DEAN. I don't believe I do.

BISHOP. You should acquaint yourself with it. *The Gift
    Relationship*. The Gift as opposed to mere economic
    exchange, this for that. I would dearly love to sit down with
    the Governor of the Bank of England or, yes, the Chancellor
    and outline Mauss's theory of *potlatch* – derived I think from
    his study of – now, were they Hopi Indians? Yes, the *potlatch*
    being an act of inordinate generosity, a great bonfire of
    goods and riotous imbibing to forge bonds of enduring
    recipricocity –

DEAN. Will you forgive me if I say I am not sure I see the
    pertinence of this?

BISHOP. The pertinence? Isn't this what we see out of this
    window – aren't Occupy with their tents and caravanserai a
    great gift to this city and this church?

DEAN. I find it hard to see it as a gift. A threat perhaps.

BISHOP. That is I think a very unfortunate reading of events.

DEAN. It may be so; but it arises out of the life and workings of
    this church, of our diocese being hindered and undermined
    on a daily basis by what seems to me an entirely contingent
    free festival that persists simply because it can, and which
    would hardly be tolerated, brooked, borne anywhere else in
    this city whatever it claims to be standing for. I'm sorry.
    Ranting again.

BISHOP. Not at all. You must give voice to your feelings. May
    I… well, may I…?

    The BISHOP *clumsily lumbers over to the* DEAN *and pulls
    him into a bear hug.*

    It has been very hard for you.

    The DEAN, *a little confused, breaks free.*

DEAN. You find you can sleep through it?

BISHOP. I am a heavy sleeper.

DEAN. That's... enviable. Now, how can I help you?

The BISHOP *unfolds a copy of the* Daily Telegraph.

BISHOP. You will of course have seen this.

DEAN. I don't take the *Telegraph*.

BISHOP. The ecclesiastical coverage is unrivalled. Yes, regrettable that George decided to weigh in.

DEAN. George?

BISHOP. Carey. Short but shall we say unconstructive think-piece.

The BISHOP *rather fastidiously tears it out and offers it to the* DEAN.

The observation about the cathedral 'losing its nerve' is uncollegiate.

DEAN. Perhaps he's missing his pre-eminence.

BISHOP. Perhaps so; elsewhere, the maunderings of the Bishop of Buckingham which I think easier to parry.

DEAN. Indeed. The Bishop of where?

BISHOP. But now with the Prime Minister demanding the reopening of the cathedral, an end to the demonstration and an end to... well – indecision we seem to be at the centre of quite a storm.

DEAN. When you say 'we' I presume you mean... 'me'.

BISHOP. The conventional logic in public relations is the story you wish to tell the media is rarely the one they want to hear. My communications team truly work miracles; even for Exxon Mobil I'm told. I can drop off their details with your – ah.

The PA *comes in with coffees.*

PA. Americano, two sugars. Flat white: no sugar.

DEAN. Many thanks, Lizzie. Yes, Lizzie's father has a living in – did you say Royston?

PA. Oh, no, Ashwell, actually. Five miles north of Royston.

BISHOP. Ashwell. Ashwell. St Mary's?

PA. That's right.

BISHOP. Splendid pilgrim's carving of Old St Paul's. Circa thirteenth century.

PA. Right. Dad always said it was fourteenth century.

BISHOP. Fourteenth? I doubt that.

PA. I guess it's just medieval graffiti; in the end. The lawyer from the City (is it Gemma?) is due imminently.

She goes.

DEAN. Lizzie has a degree in history – in all but name.

BISHOP. Do you think she might be overqualified? We get graduates for even the most menial tasks these days. Not given to humility.

DEAN. Other than for pastoral reasons for which I am always grateful why did you drop by?

BISHOP. It's not my role to direct or impose. But I did wonder if there was anything to place in the balance – given I am bidden to Lambeth?

DEAN. Ah. You're seeing Rowan.

BISHOP. Just a catch-up, now he's back in the saddle.

I merely wondered if there was anything you'd like me to convey?

DEAN. Nothing I couldn't convey myself in my own good time.

BISHOP. I see.

DEAN. Is this is about the Canon Chancellor?

BISHOP. I don't approve of Twitter. I find the character limit impels one towards glibness. Blogging as you know I delight in.

But clearly... for you, here, now. We are in a new game. I had presumed his going might have made your stance clearer.

The bells ring for ten o'clock.

DEAN. Will you join us – for Eucharist?

BISHOP. Oh. Eucharist? Well, will I be able to?

DEAN. You would of course be very welcome.

Now, I rather need to turn my attention to my sermon.

BISHOP. I see. You *are* reopening.

DEAN. Do you think it inappropriate for me to give the homily?

BISHOP. Oh. It is not liturgically necessary. Fierce attention will be placed upon every word you speak.

DEAN. All the more necessity then. To speak.

BISHOP. It is, as you know, your service.

We all need to make decisions of shining clarity from now on.

The BISHOP*'s mobile goes; ringtone Tavener's 'The Protecting Veil'.*

Excuse me. (*Into phone.*) Yes, yes, hello, yes, I will be with you imminently.

He slurps his coffee and puts on his coat.

(*To* DEAN.) I am not sure what the fuss is all about – with these flat whites. An Antipodean thing, I believe. Well. I leave not entirely empty-handed. What was it Luther said? If the world were to end tomorrow, I would plant a tree. Such a humorous man; we forget this.

The BISHOP *goes.*

The DEAN *sits heavily, facing away from us, staring out of the window. Is he praying? From outside a low samba begins, chants, whistles, waves of applause.*

The PA *comes in.*

PA. Knock, knock. I hope that's not overly tentative.

Pause.

I just meant… nothing. That lawyer lady needs to leave us in time for the meet – at the Guildhall is it? – Special Meeting of the Transport and Planning Committee, 10.45 –

DEAN. A foregone conclusion.

PA. Right. So, she's seeking confirmation of chapter's position.

With regard to Occupy.

Pause.

DEAN. I think we all… yes.

He stands, slightly crumples.

PA. Are you all right?

DEAN. Slight… giddiness… nothing.

Pause.

PA. Did you er, did you manage to get any breakfast?

DEAN. Breakfast? Actually I think I may have forgotten to.

Pause.

PA. Well, look, I bring in my own – it's not –

She goes to her rucksack pulls out some plastic cartons.

A banana: slow-release energy. Plus I made flapjack.

DEAN. Oh. No. That's kind.

PA. You'd be doing me a favour; I burned the flapjack.

The DEAN *eats some flapjack. Sips his coffee.*

DEAN. The wind was out of the east last night, down the Thames, like a banshee. You hear this – the drumming, the music, the occasional shout. Normally this part of London falls mute after dark. A siren, boats on the river, but no traffic, few voices. Just the bells. As if one was in a retreat. But since they came, every night this fitful rhythm of noise, shouts, cries – are they in pain? Is it laughter?

Pause.

PA. What will you speak to?

DEAN. I am out of practice. Two weeks without preaching. Well. The glory of the lectionary is I have little choice, little latitude to rant. The Feast of St Simon and St Jude. Of whom we know next to nothing.

PA. Pretty unpromising material.

DEAN. 'Jude: patron saint of hopeless causes. Jude: martyred in "inhospitable lands".' The sum total of my notes.

I am not known for my oratory. I acknowledge the shortcoming. But I wish to speak today – to admit we that committed a great error; to admit this is the first time in weeks I've looked in the mirror without flinching.

The bells ring the quarter-hour.

Thank you again for the refreshments.

PA. Absolutely. Absolutely. Oh, there's the – the stuff you asked for.

She lays out some documents, goes. The DEAN *finds a Bible. He leafs through.*

DEAN. 'There are some saints who come down to us with complete biographies.'

He writes a note.

'From the pages of the Bible we can actually experience the life, work and journeys of St Paul; but today we celebrate two Apostles of Jesus, Simon and Jude, whose life stories are virtually unknown to us.'

The soil is broken, the water gushes… from the source.

The PA *re-enters.*

PA. I know I'm not permitted to apologise –

The DEAN *holds up his hands. He checks the Bible and the lectionary.*

DEAN. John, 15, verse 17: Jesus said to his disciples, 'If the world hates you, be aware that it hated me before it hated you. If you belonged to the world, the world would love you as its own. Because you do not belong to the world, because I have chosen you out of the world therefore the world hates you.'

'You do not belong to the world.'

It reads us as much as we read it.

The CITY LAWYER, *dazzling, shock of hair, expensive dress, comes in.*

CITY LAWYER. Was I not meant to come in?

DEAN. Not at all. Good morning. Gemma?

CITY LAWYER. That's right – well done. Just a quick heads-up.

En route to the Guildhall. Okay. I bought cake. Don't ask why, just a whim, saw them in the window of Maison Blanc and thought, 'Buy cake, Gemma.' Didn't even ask as to what the – actually what sort of cakes are these?

PA. Cupcakes, I guess.

CITY LAWYER. On some insanely greedy impulse I bought five. Please – pitch in!

DEAN. I had resolved to resist cakes, pastries and the like.

CITY LAWYER. Worthy resolutions are suspended in a crisis. Essential fat and caffeine! I'll just leave them there.

Right. So, gosh, poor you. Losing Barbara now. Hard act to follow. And now your Canon Chancellor. Slightly like a Poirot – who will they get next? What an atrocious fortnight you have had. God, is it even that?

DEAN. Fourteen days as of today. Each as long as a year.

The DEAN *takes a cake.*

Do we think this is lemon?

PA. Banoffee. Probably.

The DEAN *replaces the cake.*

CITY LAWYER. So it seemed appropriate that we broke bread over our… situation ahead of today's meet, commencing in – OMG – forty minutes. I take it you got my PowerPoint?

PA. It was received.

CITY LAWYER. Okay. Was it discussed, minuted?

Pause. The DEAN *is at the window.*

PA. It was felt to be… inadmissible.

CITY LAWYER. Really? Would have thought it might have been of assistance to you – in your deliberations.

DEAN. You mentioned a meeting?

CITY LAWYER. Yes, yes: the Special Meeting of the Transport and Planning Committee. Which despite the modest name has a fairly major concern – our uninvited guests out there.

DEAN. Ah. You refer to Occupy. Periphrastically.

CITY LAWYER. Yes. Actually given that, would you mind walking me through your managerial grid so I can speak with authority to that – they love the power-list stuff.

DEAN. I'm sorry?

CITY LAWYER. Oh you know I, Gemma, am part of a legal team reporting up to a tier of management within the Corporation, the Town Clerk, the Chamberlain, the Remembrancer, all the sub-departments, the City Surveyor,

Secondary of London and Under Sheriff... all ultimately answerable to the Lord Mayor: I mean it's baroque stuff –

PA. Presumably intentionally.

CITY LAWYER. I don't think we've been introduced.

PA. Oh, no, I'm new – Lizzie. Hi. Look, should I buzz off?

DEAN. Lizzie is a history graduate.

PA. History and politics. Technically I didn't... graduate –

CITY LAWYER. Well, that's fine. Fine. I suppose they'll need to know who wears the trousers here. As opposed to the skirts!

DEAN. Well, I am the nominal head.

CITY LAWYER. Great. And your line manager is...?

DEAN. My line manager? I presume we're not including the Deity in this... schema.

CITY LAWYER. Surely there's someone above you a little closer to the ground? The Bishop of London, say? The Archbishop? The PM perhaps?

DEAN. We are an authority unto ourselves. Not unlike the City in that respect.

CITY LAWYER. Oh. Ha. Touché. So the next question is who's liable? Essentially who do I sue were I minded to? But I think of course you've answered me on that already – I sue you; if I come to harm on your premises; if harm occurs on your premises that impacts on me; if my property is damaged inadvertently or otherwise, or my economic activity hindered, say: I would sue you, the Dean of St Paul's.

DEAN. Put so baldly – it's quite... disconcerting.

Pause. The CITY LAWYER *checks her phone.*

PA. But if I may, there was a sense – in the meeting – it was felt, that whilst it would be unwise to ignore the Corporation's position on this – you – they – actually have no power to compel us – the Church – to one course of action or another. I mean, Mr Dean, would that be a fair summary?

CITY LAWYER. Oh, no direct power, no. But I hardly need to remind you St Paul's sits within the City of London which constitutes a body autonomous from the wider polity of London and to some extent even UK PLC; and you hardly need reminding that within that square mile are located some of the highest net-worth enterprises on the planet, that it is the duty of everyone within the Corporation to defend and represent the interests of these enterprises, on the global stage and within this – nation – and – it goes without saying – what is taking place out there, what is occurring – out there – is occurring within our jurisdiction. And were it to – occur – for any further extended period of time –

DEAN. Exactly what land lies within your jurisdiction? Sorry; I interrupted you.

CITY LAWYER. No, no, you are the Dean of St Paul's after all!

DEAN. What land lies within your jurisdiction and what within ours?

And would such a jurisdiction override, well, certain historical rights – the right, say, to protest?

Pause.

CITY LAWYER. Whew – fundamental stuff – sort of at the eleventh hour, but – well, can I just say we totally accept the right to protest, totally. We have no clue what the mission of this – gathering – amounts to, what they hope to achieve. But we also have a responsibility to uphold public law, by-laws, self-evidently we do. It's generally agreed we've been very restrained I think, a fortnight in.

DEAN. We struggled a little on that – the pertinent by-laws.

CITY LAWYER. Well as I said I did send over the relevant attachments.

DEAN. Isn't there something about an attachment which falls short of genuine explanation and well, advocacy?

CITY LAWYER. Okay, well, very quickly indeed, there are a number of clear breaches of statute the gathering could be dispersed under Part IV of the Serious Organised Crime and

Police Act 2005; or perhaps even Section 14 (1) of the Public
Order Act of 1986; but this would be deploying a power tool
to crack a pistachio. Our sense is we should begin with
reference to Section 130 of the Highways Act 1980, with
particular reference to subsection three thereof, namely 'the
Highways Public Authority is required to prevent as far as
possible the stopping-up or obstruction of (a) the highways
for which they are the public authority or (b) any highway
for which they are not the Highway Authority, if in their
opinion the stopping-up or obstruction of that highway
would be prejudicial to the interests of their area.' And I
think we in the City have concluded that yes, this –
happening – is now indeed prejudicial to our interests.

DEAN. You seem very sure of that. In advance of your...
meeting.

CITY LAWYER. So; if we were to decide to go to the courts to
get such an injunction do we go in step with you: St Paul's?

Pause.

I mean would that be your understanding? Mr Dean?

The DEAN *looks at the blueprints and documents on the
table. The bells ring the half-hour.*

DEAN. The crux is surely ownership: which land pertains to
your and which to our... jurisdiction? Which is of a rather
older and higher order.

CITY LAWYER. I think the City might precede the cathedral in
fact. Ninth century?

DEAN. We've been on this site since 604. Anno Domini.

CITY LAWYER. Okay, okay. I have ten minutes if I literally
run... but I bow to your – okay, fine, I think we – I have
that... somewhere.

*She brings up on her tablet a map of the cathedral and
adjacent streets.*

As you know we've leased Paternoster Square to Mitsubishi
holdings but of course we still have duty of care to that land;

we own the North Churchyard, much of the South
Churchyard, we clearly oversee everything up to New
Change and down to Ludgate Hill – the hatched area – okay?

PA. So, if I may – so the tents are mainly in this area here, up to
and including the cathedral steps, the Queen Anne
monument, the steps down to the crypt, et cetera, et cetera,
and that bit's effectively under St Paul's – jurisdiction.

CITY LAWYER. Well, I think maybe nine of the tents are on St
Paul's land; this area is in fact a public highway –

PA. But – sorry – to press the point; can these by-laws be acted
upon without the consent of both landowners?

DEAN. The landowners presumably need to act, what's the
phrase – in concert – wouldn't they, for any action?

CITY LAWYER. Ooh, is it just me or is this meeting starting to
veer off on a slightly odd tangent? Why, why would we not
act in concert? I thought this is what you met to confirm last
night thus provoking your troublesome Canon to pack his
bags. Or was he sent packing?

DEAN. Nobody, nobody sent anyone packing as a point of fact.

CITY LAWYER. Okay. Fine. My apologies.

The DEAN *is at the window.*

DEAN. St Paul's Cross; in the North Churchyard. Do you see it?

The source of the City itself; from Norman times, perhaps
earlier, records suggest a folk-meet occurred here; a people's
parliament if you like! In the Reformation era firebrands
would preach against usury, against merchants in the very
presence of the Mayor. Doubtless also a riotous affair – we
find it mentioned in Stow's *Survey of London*. Lizzie, you
found the relevant –

PA. Yes. Okay, so, yeah: 'The citizenry of London would meet
to determine their mind on divers affairs… er… all freemen
might speak fearless of censure.'

DEAN. A tradition of free, even odious utterance. Of untrammelled public speech. It's resonant isn't it, to think of it in this context?

CITY LAWYER. Oh highly... resonant.

CITY LAWYER *checks her phone again.*

DEAN. Yet we are so parochial in time. Crossing the square this morning in the mist, the sleepers in their tents, I had this intimation of the past: what if with rights of sanctuary and the confusions between the footprint of the pre-Wren St Paul's and our present one, what if with the long tradition of public dissent on this spot – what if no one has legal suzerainty over this land?

CITY LAWYER. Yeah, I'm now due at the Guildhall in five minutes.

DEAN. Gemma, law badly made is no law at all, you surely know that. Convey to the meeting that our friends outside have pitched camp on a legal sinkhole. That they know it too; should we not place our actions in the light of history?

CITY LAWYER. Well as the song goes I may not know much about that but I have a pretty good sense of the immediate present. I think we all hope this will melt away and soon and the law proper may never need to be used. But let's not forget we have a duty of care to the workers and citizens of this borough, and both of our great organisations are liable for the well-being, spiritual and otherwise of the general public. You know if it weren't for the tents they could stay!

DEAN. You seem set on eviction.

CITY LAWYER. I don't believe anyone used the word 'eviction'.

DEAN. They'll hardly go meekly – listen to them. They are dug in. They've had enough of meekness.

They'll have to be made to go; how's that likely to happen?

At dawn: as we expel the Romany, the migrants? Tear gas and pepper spray? How will the City look then? How will London look then?

The CITY LAWYER *starts packing away.*

CITY LAWYER. I'm sorry. I came here to sign off on a conversation, really. And my role is always only to advise.

DEAN. And what would you say was the status of your advice?

CITY LAWYER. Non-statutory. But I would very strongly advise you not to engage with the people out there in any form and join us, today, in our lawful attempt to stop them choking the life out of this great City with their scruffy, illiterate and unsightly sit-in.

DEAN. A very considerable overstatement.

CITY LAWYER. In the eyes of the law dialogue implies consent; they know that. There are some very smart legal minds out there. Recognise one or two from my old chambers. Any resistance on your part to our plans will be read as consent to the continuance of the camp's existence, even connivance with its aims. Everything we do is broadcast to the entire world, every little thing. Oh, what's the ermm... the gallery? The whispering gallery is it? Bit like that. Everything amplified, everything analysed and interpreted, every whisper reverberating round the world. Now, will you, the Church, back the Corporation if it seeks for an injunction to begin proceedings that may, yes, in the fullness of time lead to an eviction?

Pause.

Mr Dean?

DEAN. We will make our own announcement at our press briefing.

CITY LAWYER. Great. Which is what... in a couple of hours?

DEAN. The briefing will take place in two hours or so, yes.

PA. Two hours and thirty minutes.

CITY LAWYER. Okay. So – what's going to change in two hours and thirty minutes?

DEAN. I suppose one lesson of this last week is a great deal might change in two hours and thirty minutes.

Pause. The bells ring the quarter-hour.

CITY LAWYER. Well, this is all very strange. The Planning and Transport Committee await us. The press await us. The world basically awaits us. Everyone, everyone is seeking clarity. Has London lost its nerve or its marbles or both? The world would urgently like to know. Okay, I have to literally run.

She notices the uneaten cakes.

Maybe I'll take those? Find a better home for them, perhaps.

She goes.

PA. I overstepped the mark again.

DEAN. I daresay you did.

PA. Never been great at boundaries. They said that at the wealth-management place. 'Don't get involved, little chavette!'

DEAN. I have always had an extremely friendly relationship with the City. The livery companies. I dine with them. I confess it can be seductive. Well, we all like ritual and good wine and suppers in panelled halls, not to mention the regalia. But of late the lustre's wearing off a little.

The VIRGER comes in.

VIRGER. So they're cleaning the steps. Occupy. Brilliant – create a royal mess and then clean it up for the cameras.

PA. Shall I rewrite the press release? In the light of our new position?

DEAN. I have a cathedral to reopen.

PA. Of course. You're the Dean.

The PA goes.

VIRGER. The Friends came in early. The Worshipful Company of Gardeners have done a fine job on the flowers. Everyone's rallying round. You can almost feel the building come back to life.

DEAN. Splendid.

VIRGER. A shadow of what it ought to be.

> I was discourteous to you. I am not one to disavow the respect owing to the clergy. You won't have had time to read it, of course, stupid.

> *He pulls the letter out; it is still unopened. He opens it. Reads.*

DEAN. We all have the very highest expectations of this building, this community. I sometimes resent Christopher Wren for that.

VIRGER. He is *the* greatest Englishman. Up there with Churchill.

> The great don't compromise. They know life's too important, God's too important, England's too important for it. That's belief in my book. This lot out here, they think putting up a tent's belief.

> And no, I'm sorry, but I don't see enough of that mettle in you... in your tenure.

DEAN. Your father was in the Night Watch I think. During the Blitz?

VIRGER. Dad? Yes, he was, yes.

DEAN. I believe they slept in the crypt.

VIRGER. I don't know if they ever slept. He was there when the high altar was hit.

DEAN. Was he? Was he indeed?

VIRGER. Lying doggo in the pitch black. Hit the great arch over the Quire. Can't imagine the noise, the great heat, falling masonry.

Yes. They walked out in the dawn, whole area was gone, this place a shell; St Paul's was unscathed. That's a miracle in my book.

DEAN. Yes.

VIRGER. Dean Matthews didn't dream of closing it for one second.

Pause.

DEAN. And you will never forgive me for doing so; I understand that, because, well, I will never forgive myself.

VIRGER. I often wonder what God makes of us, I do. I wonder if he finds us contemptible. I think I would if I were God.

The DEAN *is very still.*

Mr Dean?

DEAN. It's strange, but – I feel – anxious. About Eucharist! I don't believe I have ever felt it before.

VIRGER. 'Sufficient unto the day', Mr Dean.

DEAN. Yes. Yes. 'Sufficient unto the day is the evil thereof.'

Matthew, 6, 34.

Would you talk me through it, Michelle? I am out of practice.

VIRGER. Well: noon. Great Tom sounds.

DEAN. Yes.

VIRGER. Everyone in place, in the nave. We open the west door – slowly.

DEAN. Very good.

VIRGER. Ensure the steps are clear, admit the public, conduct them to their seats.

DEAN. The vestments?

VIRGER. The chasuble, with cowl, over the cassock alb. I thought we'd do you in here so you could progress in your full display –

DEAN. Very good. Provisions for communion?

VIRGER. Six chalices, wafers in the ciborium, credence table set, red front cloth on the altar.

DEAN. And the choir enter –

VIRGER. The choir enter; led by crucifer, canons in order of eminence. Will the Canon Chancellor be amongst them? Such incredible anger at him, I'll find it very hard to do the Peace with him if and when the time comes. I must say I am finding the whole business of forgiveness extremely challenging.

DEAN. The Welcome.

VIRGER. The hymn. Not forgetting the Prayer for Purity.

DEAN. And – the homily.

VIRGER. You're set on that?

DEAN. I know it is not liturgically called for. I know you think it inappropriate. I know how far I fall short of my predecessors but, Michelle, today we must speak in clear words to the world about what has transpired, about what we are here for. So, with your indulgence, I will preach. I believe even my great predecessors would have approved. I hope I have your support in this.

Pause.

VIRGER. We'll set out the legilium on the floor under the dome.

DEAN. Thank you. Thank you.

The bells ring for eleven o'clock.

VIRGER. Crossed the Millennium Bridge coming in. First bus before the crowds. Cleaners coming off shift at Canary Wharf. Not a word of English spoken, which I find relaxes me now. No tourists or city workers. Low sun. You step on that bridge, lifted up above the river. There between the buildings, there it is. Cupola, stone lantern, cross flashing in the light. Almost thought I heard trumpets, tears in my eyes from the wind.

DEAN. Yes. 'Resurgam' – Wren carved it on the south transept.

It's indestructible, Michelle. Indestructible. Because you are the temple, we all are. Will you allow me to return this?

He offers the letter; she doesn't take it.

Well – let us ready ourselves for our congregation.

The VIRGER *goes; the* DEAN *alone. He stands; then, he kneels and begins to pray.*

The PA *enters, sees him, is not sure what to do. Starts to leave.*

Does your father do this?

PA. Dad?

DEAN. Does he pray? In the vulgar sense of prayer, the everyday sense?

PA. I've seen him at – prayer.

DEAN. What might he pray for?

PA. Oh, stuff; you know: 'Oh Lord please let Lizzie not take recreational drugs or fraternise with the more sexually promiscuous village boys'; 'Oh Lord may she find in herself the wisdom to not take Media Studies at A level'; 'Oh Lord please prevent my wife from inspecting my ill-conceived pension plans.'

The DEAN *doesn't laugh.*

DEAN. Divine guidance often enters in very late in the tale. One thinks of Abraham shaking with fear, the knife at Isaac's white throat before reprieve arrives.

Silence.

I wonder if you might have any further advice… yourself?

PA. Me?

DEAN. I sense a kind of wisdom in you that seems to elude me today.

PA. Wisdom! I don't think so.

DEAN. Perhaps you are a vehicle for His will. You understand these people out there: the young, disinherited, disenfranchised. Yes, what would you advise me to do? Were I to ask?

PA. I mean – how am I even qualified to – ?

DEAN. Nobody is. Nobody is qualified. In the end.

The BISHOP *re-enters.*

BISHOP. Had to get the cabbie to drop me at Bank and walk from there. Moronic, truculent crowds. Am I interrupting something?

The PA *walks out.*

Are you... unwell?

The DEAN *stands.*

DEAN. I was praying. Is that so strange?

BISHOP. Not strange at all.

Pause.

DEAN. A good meeting with Rowan?

BISHOP. I hardly think 'good' describes it.

DEAN. I expect I came up.

I mean I expect my many shortcomings came up.

BISHOP. Oh come, Mr Dean.

DEAN. I find I am in no mood for games today. I find I am impatient, yes, with conceits and subterfuges and the tacit, all of the ways we tend to do things, which I am starting to see as plainly evil –

BISHOP. You know the whereabouts of the Canon Chancellor?

DEAN. He has to all intents and purposes vanished.

BISHOP. I think that unlikely, don't you?

DEAN. So your question was rhetorical.

BISHOP. I happen to know he spoke with Rowan.

DEAN. I am fond of the Archbishop but his lack of support for us this last fortnight has been notable.

BISHOP. Well, to be fair he's been in Assisi.

DEAN. Assisi. Wish I could have been there with him.

BISHOP. What were the exact grounds for his departure, the Canon Chancellor?

DEAN. Why ask? It's all on social media.

BISHOP. To his credit he just tweeted something to the effect that he has nothing but love and support for his colleagues.

DEAN. Another tweet! He's always been prolific, that's why I appointed him. I however am not prolific – is that a weakness? You, and he, and all my predecessors here have been people shall we say of the book, leaving your trace everywhere as if somehow you fear by not constantly producing a fine spray of comment you might cease to exist. I take a different view – I disappear gladly into my robes and ministry and my deepest hope is not to be remembered other than by that ministry.

BISHOP. I concur with almost nothing he thinks or says but better to have him micturating from within the tent than from without.

DEAN. Oh the less said about tents and micturating the better.

BISHOP. What happened? Between you. You need to tell me.

The bells ring the quarter-hour.

DEAN. Chapter met last night. Chapter recognised that the current situation was untenable. Chapter acknowledged that the pressure upon us and on our community and yes, on the Corporation of London itself has become insupportable.

BISHOP. A judgement unanimously arrived at?

DEAN. You don't expect me to disclose confidential details.

BISHOP. This is rather bigger than us now. Our old exquisite ways are not serving us well. What were the terms of the debate? And your part in it?

The CANON CHANCELLOR *enters, coatless.*

CANON CHANCELLOR. You can say 'speak of the devil' if you like.

Just no jibes about prodigal sons; too long in the tooth for that.

DEAN. The Canon Chancellor felt he could not continue on his journey of faith alongside us.

CANON CHANCELLOR. Such a gift for euphemism.

DEAN. We hoped we might handle his going with discretion but now that seems impossible.

CANON CHANCELLOR. Stick a toe outside this panic room you'd know why I did that.

BISHOP. May we cease this undignified baiting?

Pause.

Hindsight is easy to invoke; but one might argue Canon Chancellor that you raised impossible expectations on Occupy's arrival; that you perhaps exceeded your role in seeming to side with the protesters against the police.

CANON CHANCELLOR. Oh. Okay, my role? So, my role was to keep worship going that was my primary *task* as Canon-in-Residence. So how do I do acquit this role with the entire City of London police force doing their Darth Vader stuff, on the steps of the building locking the congregation out –

BISHOP. Well, leave that aside, then, then the closure – which was an impossible situation – a cleft stick –

CANON CHANCELLOR. Even now I don't believe we did that!

DEAN. At the time of the decision I remember you were both supportive.

BISHOP. I'm glad you found me to be so; truly a devil's choice.

CANON CHANCELLOR. The thing is, Mr Dean, your fear
was – is – infectious.

BISHOP. Now look, okay, what's hard to make clear to the
latte-swilling secularists is we, the Church are practising
exactly the kind of direct democracy they claim to be
pioneering… do I, the Bishop, hold sway over the chapter
here? Of course not. Do you the Dean impose against all
odds your views and values?

DEAN. You're distancing yourself, aren't you? From that
decision.

CANON CHANCELLOR. 'Resiling' from it. Was that Blair's
word?

BISHOP. May we attempt to maintain a little more dignity in
our dealings here?

DEAN. Can we then own our decisions and stand firmly by
them?

CANON CHANCELLOR. 'What would Jesus do?' they ask –
not such a naff question.

DEAN. Oh, I think Jesus would place worship over gesture, I
think Jesus would recognise that the Church's holy work is
as vital as their callow questions.

CANON CHANCELLOR. Aren't they in fact highly relevant
questions? Does not Christ himself ask these same callow
questions of the moneylenders in the temple? 'Ye have made
it a den of thieves.'

DEAN. I suspect any thieves in the vicinity are to be found in
the care of our friends outside –

CANON CHANCELLOR. Unworthy of you, unworthy.

BISHOP. Look whatever anybody thinks, you have to admit we,
every one one of us, the entire Church is looking pretty
bloody foolish!

Pause.

Now what if we sought a new covenant? Yes, with those poor souls out there? What if we offered our own spectacular act of generous engagement, our own *potlatch*? To confound this sense that we have lined up with the calculators, those who make money their deity, those who stand against human flourishing?

DEAN. I'm sorry. I'm a little slow today... what, what are you proposing?

BISHOP. Let us go amongst them; let us break bread with them.

CANON CHANCELLOR. Bit late in the day for a charm offensive.

DEAN. They came to protest at the London Stock Exchange, a valid aim, but they were diverted, kettled into this square and so they stayed put with us, a rather softer target – and how fortunate for them that their assault on one drab enemy rebounded onto another more photogenic one.

CANON CHANCELLOR. Such a jaundiced account of such a joyous thing.

DEAN. Was it ever our choice to be the parish church of high finance? No. This spot was the beginning of London, this church has stood on this spot for a millennium, before any bank or stock exchange, before capitalism itself – and yes, they came and they built their citadels around us and so yes, we serve them as we would any neighbour – and besides who are Occupy?

CANON CHANCELLOR. Oh dreamers, exiles. Akin to the early church, perhaps.

DEAN. You know that's a fatuous comparison.

CANON CHANCELLOR. People of courage, people burning their boats, teaching assistants, postmen, even met an ex-hedge-fund manager amongst them.

DEAN. But are they a political party with rules, members, a constitution? For anyone not present how are they

answerable? So, fine, you say 'engage', but with whom
exactly?

CANON CHANCELLOR. Go to their assemblies? Speak at
their forum?

DEAN. We have spoken to them, and each time we speak we
are obliged to speak to another of them, as if somehow
speaking itself was a corruption, and anything we seem to
agree is overridden at what they call General Assembly but
what I can only see as people bawling into bullhorns –

CANON CHANCELLOR. And isn't that a tiny bit exciting,
invigorating?

DEAN. No, no, it's as if one were to speak to the sea, to speak
to a crowd from Westminster Bridge, to write in the air itself
– so yes, engage fine, fine, if I felt there were matters of
substance real changes but this, what you propose is merely
appearance management –

BISHOP. Then accept that we live amongst shadows not
substances! That we cannot neglect how we appear at these
windows, that we appear increasingly like some dithering
costume drama of faith, aligned with the very powerful
against the very weakest.

Pause.

With the Canon Chancellor amongst you, the chapter was a
perfectly balanced equilibrium of the progressive and the
traditional, looking forward and back, left and right – with
him gone you appear an institution concerned with little but
its own longevity in a world on fire.

Pause.

CANON CHANCELLOR. What's this all been about, forever,
since Christ: the prophets against the priests – yeah, the
priests keep the temple clean, wear the frocks, expel the
women, the menses, the dirt, and they love all that, but then
the prophets come right in and what do they do, what do they
do, they pull the temple down, right – Samson, Isaiah, Jesus,

Paul, Luther, Calvin – pull the fucker right down – and right now the priests are hiding, hiding in the temple and no, I'm not saying I am in the prophets' company in any shape or form I'm not saying that!

Pause.

BISHOP. I can only suggest when you meet the press you stand with me and announce a new, some new – initiative – you outflank the cynics and the wreckers, and thereby refresh the meaning of our vocation. Some great change must happen here. Some *defining* change.

Either that, or, well, perhaps a rethink. Of your... position.

DEAN. I'm sorry. Are you suggesting – implying – that I – what? – that I resign?

BISHOP. I don't believe I said any such thing.

Pause.

DEAN. Well. Well, that would certainly be another first. Yes. The first Dean to close the building; the first to walk away from it in post.

BISHOP. As you know do I have any power to force your hand one way or the other, none at all. I... I... you – presumably – need to prepare for Eucharist.

And none of this alters my great personal... my great –

DEAN. Sssh!

Pause.

BISHOP. I continue to pray for you.

The BISHOP *goes. Silence.*

CANON CHANCELLOR. Sort of hoped we might be made of sterner stuff. Than this.

You know what... sorry. Just being in here. Been – oh – been quite a... morning. Sorry.

Now he's weeping. The PA *comes in, clocks them; the* DEAN *waves her away.*

No absolution for Judas, eh?

DEAN. It's hardly my role; to absolve you.

CANON CHANCELLOR. No. Man up! Besides who's Judas here? The one leaving or the one staying put? Anyway I have a lot of time for Judas.

DEAN. He was a zealot too.

CANON CHANCELLOR. Perfectly valid position.

DEAN. In 33AD perhaps.

The bells ring the half-hour.

CANON CHANCELLOR. I know how my conduct must have been – perceived; how it probably – felt –

DEAN. You have your public.

CANON CHANCELLOR. Was that… sarcasm?

DEAN. Am I ever sarcastic?

CANON CHANCELLOR. No. You never are. You never are. Marks you out.

DEAN. I expect you feared the meaning of your gesture might have been upstaged by subsequent events.

CANON CHANCELLOR. My 'gesture'. Oh yes. Cut it down to size.

DEAN. Nor was I attempting to do that.

CANON CHANCELLOR. Actually will you please stop mollifying me? Will you please stop being so predictably kind and accommodating and giving, because you know where has that led us?

DEAN. Nothing you can say to me is harsher than my own account.

CANON CHANCELLOR. Look at you, doing it again, you can't help yourself! This is what they hate about the Church isn't it? Always ready to take the punches, lap up the punishment, apparently immune to what makes real people breathe harder – for once say what you think of me!

The DEAN *is stunned.*

DEAN. Very well; very well; you betrayed my trust – is that what you wish to hear?

CANON CHANCELLOR. Yes. Thank you. Well done. Very mild.

DEAN. Very well, and when, when one's trust is gone it does not return easily.

CANON CHANCELLOR. Oh this is milky stuff.

DEAN. Yes, fine, and as now I have felt all too often your contempt for me and do you know I think there's something actually rather elitist in that –

CANON CHANCELLOR. Bouncing off me, blanks, all blanks –

DEAN. – and I think you care rather too much about what the world thinks of you and yes, that perhaps you are vain, vain, vain. Vain. You are a vain man.

Pause.

Feel free to – to reciprocate –

CANON CHANCELLOR. Okay; I find you are quick to take comfort in the mediocre, and that your unshakeable decency may simply stem from a failure in imagination, oh, and that perhaps you were better suited to the Diocese of the Isle of Man and Sodor than that of the greatest city in the world.

Pause.

DEAN. These were long-contemplated words. With real heat in them. Real… venom.

Pause.

I think it might make sense if you left this room and perhaps if we could for the period of your notice maintain a healthy distance.

CANON CHANCELLOR. Right.

DEAN. I really need to get on. Cathedral to open, press to manage, kittens to drown – ah, even sarcasm now, look at me.

CANON CHANCELLOR. Finally dragged you down to my level.

DEAN. Go. Please.

The CANON CHANCELLOR *looks broken.*

CANON CHANCELLOR. What am I now? Free? Vindicated? How long can you live on vindication? Am I behaving incredibly erratically?

DEAN. In due course you'll acquire a living of some sorts.

CANON CHANCELLOR. I'm not vicar material! I'm not cut out for the pastoral role, I've never pretended that, for God's sake I did a PhD on Nietzsche, would you come to me for help? Huh?

Finally they laugh.

I confess fully I am wilful, I'm skittish, you know this, you, you're a rock –

DEAN. In the Irish Sea by all accounts.

CANON CHANCELLOR. Look at me, tweeting away, such *bullshit*, yet you feel you must and there was a palpable roar, as if I'd loosed an arrow into a crowd, I had to get away – from here – literally ran across Millennium Bridge, into the press of the crowd, bolted into Tate Modern, sat in the caff just to get my breath, switched on my phone, almost jumped out of my hands, seething with requests, questions, abusive threads – why does the Catholic Herald hate me so much?

Walk upriver to Lambeth to see... Rowan. He said almost nothing, as per usual, he is, I contend, a very holy man, like

you, what am I then, the holy fool? You know all the time
you know what keeps coming back to me: Satan, in Milton:
'Better to reign in hell than to serve in heaven'?

How fucked up is that?

All the time walking back along Fleet Street, up Ludgate Hill,
there it is – watching me, finding me wanting – No, your logic
is impeccable; now I've gone, fine, let that logic prevail.

DEAN. You need me here to make your stance mean
something. You have cast me in my role. Make the error.
Then step away.

CANON CHANCELLOR. What?

DEAN. The goat taking on the sins, beaten from the village.

Yes.

CANON CHANCELLOR. Getting a bit Holman Hunt aren't
you?

DEAN. Yes.

They are still.

CANON CHANCELLOR. You know what I would very much
like – I would very much like to join you for Eucharist. How
would you feel… about that?

DEAN. Of course. You are still in the chapter. Until your notice
is served. We face the world today as a church.

CANON CHANCELLOR. This is generous of you. Incredibly
generous.

The CANON CHANCELLOR *collapses into his arms. A
moment.*

DEAN. Go and ready yourself.

The CANON CHANCELLOR *stands.*

CANON CHANCELLOR. Yeah.

The CANON CHANCELLOR *goes.*

The DEAN *alone opens the sash window – the sounds of a regular chant drift in and a samba rhythm; whistles adjoin it. The bells ring the quarter-hour. He closes the window again. The* PA *re-enters.*

DEAN. I was happy in the Isle of Man; largely because of the sound of the sea. Something of that sound here too, the morning, as the city starts up.

I didn't seek this post, I was sounded out; the letter came for me in a brown envelope. I thought it was from the Inland Revenue! But then I knew; and I had no doubt whatsoever; if the Church wished me to serve St Paul's, it would be arrogant of me to disavow their wish. That is the meaning of vocation, I think.

I shouldn't have placed that pressure on you. Soliciting your advice. Despite what I said, this is absolutely a job, nothing more.

PA. Too late. I wrote something.

DEAN. There was no need to write anything.

PA. Okay, I happen to think they're, Occupy, whilst I find them deeply annoying – their analysis is – spot-on. Spot-on.

DEAN. Right.

PA. Because I've no argument with capitalism as such but isn't it meant to work, finally?

DEAN. All this is, very, well… rhetorical isn't it?

PA. You *solicited* my advice. This is my advice.

DEAN. Yes. Sorry.

PA. Isn't this basically a colony – the City of London? I don't know who it's for. The one per cent and their flunkies. In they come and out they go, shuffling digits about, which might be okay if they added something to our happiness but they just subtract from it, no, worse, they feed off unhappiness, and what makes that even worse is their incredible unhappiness themselves! Arriving in the dawn like the dead, leaving in the dark like thieves. And I guess Occupy are just saying, 'Can we look at this, perhaps?'

And I really don't think you have the answers to their questions in here.

DEAN. Well, thank you… that's helpful.

PA. Okay. I don't think it was. Very.

Actually you know what, I haven't finished.

DEAN. Oh.

PA. My dad – okay – my dad, the guy I see most days sat in his crumpled PJs watching rubbish sitcoms, avoiding sex with Mum – basically a total human car crash – isn't he a fundamentally different person from the man I see in church, the one up in the pulpit – doesn't that other person sort of float free from my dad? That man is loved, revered, he takes part in mysteries I actually really wish I could… share, every week, every day he brings together the living and the dead.

And that, all that, out there, it's just a bit human, a bit limited, isn't it, in comparison? Out there's not is not where you're called to live is it?

I don't really know what I'm saying, and I so want to apologise but I can't –

DEAN. Lizzie, no, it's fine, that was –

PA. – and okay I got a text from Gemma. The City voted 'yes' – to eviction. Well. To proceed to an injunction and so on.

DEAN. I see.

PA. Basically she needs to know if St Paul's is on board.

DEAN. Yes; we are 'on board'.

PA. That's what you want to say? You'll seek an injunction?

DEAN. Yes.

PA. Fine. You'll seek an injunction and in time, an eviction?

I mean, this is what God wants you to do is it?

DEAN. God's will is not to be known directly, or immediately.
But I feel His hand in the small of my back, shoving me into
the dark wings. Go. Make the bad choice, the only choice
you can make, the choice that comes from the person you
have come to be, not the person others might wish you to be.

PA. I'm sorry but, really, the way – the way you talk, I don't
know – as if all this was somehow inevitable.

The DEAN *can't speak.*

I honestly don't believe that, don't get that.

DEAN. Well. I need hardly say you're young, need I?

Text Gemma to the effect that we 'march in step'.

Please.

The bells ring for midday.

The VIRGER *enters with the vestments, a chasuble, with
cowl, and a cassock alb with two* CHORISTERS *of about
ten. They are in robes and ruffs and look immaculate but
have trainers on underneath.*

What, what's this?

She sounds a tuning fork. They sing.

CHORISTERS.
When thou, O Christ, didst send the Twelve,
Thy work of grace to do,
Conjoined in holy bands of love
They went forth, two and two.

Today, O Lord, before us here
Two blest Apostles stand,
Forever in Thy realm above
United hand in hand.

Jude bids us in our holy faith
With zeal to seek the right,
And zeal shines brightly in the name,
Simon the Canaanite.

So send Thou down into our hearts
Thy Spirit from above,
And give us ever-fervent zeal
Tempered with holy love.

And may we with these servants then
In heav'nly glory be!
For fellowship in holy love
Is unity in Thee.

The DEAN *has tears in his eyes; he applauds as does everyone else.*

DEAN. Who are these cherubim?

VIRGER. Tell the Dean your names, boys.

CHORISTER ONE. Oh. I'm Jude.

CHORISTER TWO. Yeah. Simon.

VIRGER. The prebend thought you'd appreciate the irony.

DEAN. Jude – and Simon – come in person to hymn me. Have we any more flapjack, Lizzie, for our Apostles?

PA. I think we have some flapjack, yes. Do you like flapjack?

CHORISTER ONE. Cool.

They fall on the biscuits.

CHORISTER TWO. Bit burnt.

DEAN. Nevertheless restorative.

Are you excited, boys? About today?

CHORISTER ONE. Will there be tons of people?

DEAN. What do you think?

CHORISTER TWO. Mum said we'd be on the news.

CHORISTER ONE. Will they like film us singing?

DEAN. The world will hear your song, yes.

The CHORISTERS *laugh.*

How did you come to be called Jude?

CHORISTER ONE. Oh. It's like today is my birthday, so obviously… my mum called me Jude.

DEAN. And where are you from?

CHORISTER ONE. Peckham.

CHORISTER TWO. I'm from Brentwood, sir.

DEAN. Have you had good birthdays?

CHORISTER ONE. We're going to Pizza Hut.

CHORISTER TWO. We're going to Pizza Express.

VIRGER. You probably better join the rest of the choir, boys.

The CHORISTERS *go.*

DEAN. Thank you, boys.

Perfect timing, Michelle. Perfect timing.

VIRGER. It was the prebend's idea; I thought it was tempting fate.

DEAN. A very pagan fear.

She carries the casock alb over.

VIRGER. I have checked this for moths and runs. Can you divest in here?

DEAN. I don't see why not. Sparing your blushes, Lizzie. Help me get this top off –

PA. Well. Shouldn't I be contacting – ?

DEAN. Given my tardiness to date she can wait a moment longer.

VIRGER. Here.

DEAN. Good.

The DEAN *bends;* VIRGER *slip the cassock alb over his head. They brush it down.*

If we can button it – my fingers – oh – they're somewhat wayward.

His hands are shaking. VIRGER *buttons for him.*

Thank you.

Then the girdle, the chasuble, the cowl.

The historical record suggest Pontius Pilate had an unusually long and fruitful tenure as prefect of a rather fly-blown province of the Roman Empire – that he maintained order and modulated between the various factions with good judgement.

It's not how we tend to remember him.

Thank you, Michelle.

The BISHOP *enters – he too is impeccable now in purple cassock a huge quasi-orthodox pectoral cross around his neck.*

BISHOP. Ah. Looking every inch the part of the Dean.

DEAN. The only part I know.

BISHOP. Yes. There's genuine excitement out there.

DEAN. As in here, as in here. I feel strangely nervous.

BISHOP. Stage fright. Not always a bad sign.

DEAN. As if it were my installation. Yes, that very feeling. Kneeling at the high altar, puny in the midst of it all.

BISHOP. I remember my enthronement. Incredible day. A specially commissioned Tavener, Vaughan Williams's 'Te Deum'.

VIRGER. Wasn't Cardinal Hume there?

BISHOP. Cardinal Hume, yes. Robert Runcie, of course.

VIRGER. And Mrs T herself.

BISHOP. Mrs T. Yes, were you not in fact virger, Michelle?

VIRGER. Oh. Junior virger. Glorious day. All London there.

BISHOP. So you may recall that nice touch, a contingent of the deaf were present, the choir signed their hymn as did I the blessing. Which didn't stop *The Church Times* rather cattily claiming I was inaccurate – in my signing. I would have thought the endeavour was the salient thing. But yes, this is my temple too you know.

DEAN. Of course, of course. You are the Bishop of London.

The CANON CHANCELLOR *comes on clean-shaven, in cassock.*

Ah.

BISHOP. Canon Chancellor – you seem to be trending again.

CANON CHANCELLOR. Shouldn't we put aside 'childish things'?

BISHOP. Oh, gladly, gladly.

CANON CHANCELLOR. You look magnificent. Mr Dean.

DEAN. And you look every inch the Canon Chancellor I was proud to appoint and work alongside.

CANON CHANCELLOR. Sounds very final.

A silence but for the bells and the clamour outside.

Well, do we walk over together?

DEAN. Why would we not?

Now a rhapsodic clangour of the ringing of the changes.

VIRGER. Gosh, they'll break those bells in half! Lord!

PA. It's like you're inside the bell itself –

BISHOP. Resurgam.

VIRGER. Great Tom.

CANON CHANCELLOR. The Banger. All the bloody bells!

They all look through the windows.

PA. The square's heaving.

The PA *turns away and starts to text. She looks at the* DEAN *in his robes. He turns and smiles, nods. She continues – and sends the text.*

DEAN. They're cheering now. It's a joyous sound, isn't it, in fact.

BISHOP. You seem very serene, Mr Dean.

DEAN. I am resolved. Resolved to do the wrong thing but resolved nevertheless.

CANON CHANCELLOR. The wrong thing?

DEAN. In the light of history perhaps. Will you join us, Lizzie?

PA. No, I'd better stay here. Ready the room for the press.

DEAN. Well. Wish me luck then.

PA. Oh yeah. I wish you a whole lot of that.

DEAN. You can be sure of this position whatever happens. I would think.

PA. That's really kind. But I don't reckon it's me. Do you?

DEAN. Perhaps not. Perhaps not.

Shall we process?

The DEAN *leads off, followed by the* BISHOP, *the* CANON CHANCELLOR, *the* VIRGER.

The PA *sits in one of the chairs facing the window; the noise builds.*

Blackout.

www.nickhernbooks.co.uk

facebook.com/nickhernbooks

twitter.com/nickhernbooks